Apples... a Bushel of Fun & Facts

by Bernice Kohn
illustrated by Roland Rodegast

Parents' Magazine Press • New York *A Finding-Out Book*

For Emily

Library of Congress Cataloging in Publication Data

Hunt, Bernice Kohn.
  Apples; a bushel of fun & facts.

  (A Finding-out book)
  Includes index.
  SUMMARY: Describes the history, cultivation,
and different varieties of the apple and includes
recipes and myths and legends associated with this
fruit.
  1. Apple—Juvenile literature. [1. Apple]
I. Rodegast, Roland. II. Title.
SB363.H85   634'.11   75-17911
ISBN 0-8193-0838-2

10 9 8 7 6 5 4 3 2

Contents

Apple History   5

The Apple Tree   13

How an Apple Grows   24

All Kinds of Apples   33

Apple Myths and Legends   44

Apples in the Kitchen   56

Index   63

Apple History

Apples are the most popular fruit in America. They are grown in almost every state of the United States. We can buy them in every market. Everybody likes to eat crunchy raw apples, applesauce, and apple pie. We bob for apples on Hallowe'en. We have such sayings as "He's the apple of his mother's eye," and "as American as apple pie."

But in spite of all that, our big, juicy, tasty apples are not native to America. They came from Southwest Asia long, long ago, and spread through China, Babylon, and Europe before they reached these shores. Apples have been known for so long that scientists have discovered, from charred remains, that people ate apples all the way back in the Stone Age.

When Julius Caesar conquered Britain more than 2,000 years ago, his army carried apples among its supplies. As these Roman soldiers threw away their apple cores, they accidentally planted the first apple trees in England. The English soon learned how to raise apples properly and they became a valued food. Much later, when the colonists left England for the New World, they took apple seeds along. The first apple tree in America was planted in the Massachusetts Bay Colony.

In 1657, Governor Peter Stuyvesant of New Amsterdam (now New York) had a small apple tree sent over from Holland. He planted it at what later became the corner of Third Avenue and 13th Street in New York City. The tree lived for many years and finally died. But it was allowed to remain on the street corner for more than 200 years from the time it was planted. It might be there still if it hadn't been knocked down accidentally by a horse-drawn wagon.

7

As the American colonies began to spread and grow, so did American apple orchards. They were especially successful in Virginia where two of the largest orchards were owned by George Washington and Thomas Jefferson.

When the pioneers in their covered wagons made their long, bumpy way across the wilderness to the West, they carried with them a treasured cargo of apple seeds and trees.

Explorers, missionaries, traders, and Indians all
helped to take apples across the continent, too.
By 1820 apples had spread from coast to coast,
and the first orchards were in blossom in
California.

Apples were a good fruit for the new country
because—unlike oranges, peaches, and other
delicate fruits—they were able to grow almost

everywhere. The colonists knew how to dry them, and how to preserve them as stewed apples, applesauce, and jelly. In a country where food was still scarce, apples were an important addition to winter meals.

The most famous apple planter of those early days was called Johnny Appleseed. His real name was John Chapman and he was born in Massachusetts in 1775. He became a missionary who traveled (some say barefoot) through the Midwest many times. He made friends with the Indians wherever he went and gave them apple seeds from the large sack he carried on his back. He planted seeds along all of his trails so that the early settlers often found apples already growing when they arrived in a new territory.

Even though, as we will discover later, these apples were not good to eat, the trees were very important, and the beautiful apple orchards of America are a living monument to Johnny Appleseed, a good man.

The Apple Tree

An apple tree is medium tall, usually twenty to thirty feet when fully grown, or about as high as a three-story house. A few kinds of apple trees grow even taller, but dwarf and crabapple trees are much smaller.

The spreading branches of the tree make up the *head*. It is usually quite round in shape, with a fine spray of delicate twigs along the sides of the branches. The trunk is fairly short and rather stocky. The bark is more gray than brown and so scaly that pieces of it often flake off.

Apple leaves are pale green, oval or egg-shaped, and they have sawtooth edges. They are from one to four inches long and their undersides are silvery and fuzzy. The leaves do

not grow opposite each other in pairs along the
two sides of a twig, but in a zigzag fashion which
is called *alternate*.

An apple tree is strong and sturdy, and looks
it. The branches are heavy and twisted, and even
the smaller limbs are husky. They have to be, for
a crop of apples is heavy and could easily break
a delicate tree.

When an apple tree is in bloom, it is both
lovely to look at and to smell. It is closely
covered with pink and white blossoms that fill
the air with sweet perfume. Apple trees belong

to the rose family. Though the two plants don't look at all alike, the fragrance of their blossoms is a reminder of the relationship.

Sometime when you are wandering along a country road, you might see a wild apple tree, one that was planted accidentally when a seed was dropped by a person or an animal. If you try to eat one of its apples, you will be in for a nasty surprise unless you are very lucky. Most of the time, the fruit of wild apple trees is sour, bitter, and hard. But it isn't wasted even if people can't enjoy it, because it is eaten by deer,

pheasants, foxes, and other animals. Since the seeds are not digested, they are left on the ground in the animals' droppings. Complete with their own little packages of fertilizer, they often root and form new trees.

The funny thing about wild apples tasting so bad is that they may have grown from the seeds of a really delicious apple that some passer-by tossed away years before. And that's why the governor of New Amsterdam imported an apple tree instead of planting seeds like everybody else. He knew that when you plant apple seeds, you never can tell what kind of apples you will get.

If you plant an ordinary bean, you will grow beans exactly like the one you planted, but if you plant an apple seed you will usually grow a different variety. The original Asiatic apple had to be highly cultivated in a special way before it became edible. People have known for thousands of years how to mix two different kinds of apples to produce a good-tasting

Oranges

pears

Peaches

hybrid— a cross between two kinds of plants. But hybrids do not breed true. That means that when you plant a hybrid seed, it will not produce fruit like the fruit it came from. If you plant all the seeds from one apple, each seed will turn into a different kind of apple tree—and most of them will bear terrible apples.

Apples are not the only hybrids. Many of our favorite fruits, vegetables, and flowers are hybrids developed by commercial growers.

grapes

beans

corn

The American settlers and pioneers knew about hybrids, but they usually planted seeds anyway because that was all they could easily carry on their long, hard journeys. Most of the time they grew very bad apples, but once in a while they got one good tree by chance and that was what they hoped for.

As soon as they got a good tree, they could grow as many like it as they wanted, and so could their friends and neighbors. They managed to do this by *grafting* instead of by planting seeds. That is the way apples for home use and for sale have always been raised.

There is more than one way to graft a tree, but a common one is by means of the *cleft*-graft. First, you cut a *scion*—a twig with several buds on it—from the kind of tree you want to grow. Whittle the lower end until it has the shape of a wedge. Now you are ready to graft the scion onto any young apple tree that has been grown from a seed.

Whittled end

Scion

Cut a branch off the seedling tree and make a two-inch split in the cut end left on the tree. Now take the wedge end of the scion and force it into the slit so that the bark is tightly up against the inner edge of the bark on the branch. This is important, because the part of the tree that grows is the layer just underneath the bark—the *cambium*. If the cambium of the scion and the cambium of the tree are kept tight against each other for a while, they will grow together permanently.

Seedling tree cut for grafting

Scion forced into slit

To make sure that the scion doesn't slip out of place, the joint is carefully sealed with grafting wax. When the graft has grown firmly attached to the tree, all of the old branches are cut off. Now the only branch left on the tree is the scion. In time, it will form a whole new head.

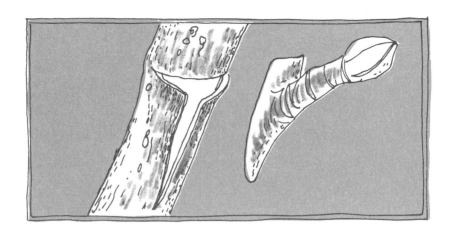

Another kind of grafting is called *budding*. For this method, you don't have to cut a scion branch. You just cut a single bud from the tree you want to reproduce and fit it into a T-shaped slit in a young seedling tree. The slit is tightly bound with cord or tape. The bud grows quickly,

and within a year
it has formed a
shoot several feet in
length. The following
year, the rest of the
tree is pruned, or cut
back to just above the
new shoot, and again,
the new growth will form
a new head.

In both kinds of
grafting, you are using
just the old roots and
trunk of the seedling
tree and starting a
new tree on top of them.

A long time ago, people who wanted to raise apples had to do their own grafting, but very few home gardeners bother to do it now. Instead, they buy young, already grafted trees from a garden center or plant nursery.

The first apple nursery in this country was started in 1730. That meant that even some of the pioneers who settled the West were able to carry young trees or scion wood with them if they had room in their wagons. Those who did were able to graft on to Johnny Appleseed's established trees and get good eating apples much more quickly than those who had to wait for a lucky tree to grow from seed.

A well-cared-for apple tree will bear fruit until it is about 40 years old. But even then, its usefulness isn't over. Apple wood is very hard and fine-grained. When a tree is chopped down, the wood is prized for carving or wood-engraving blocks, and it is often used for ax and saw handles.

How an Apple Grows

When an apple tree blooms, the blossoms grow in clusters at the end of each twig. Each cluster is surrounded by a ring of very pale, soft leaves. Both the flowers and the leaves come from buds produced the season before and protected over the winter by fuzzy scales. As the flower buds burst open, the scales drop off. When they do, they leave a small collection of lines or ridges close together on the twig. If you count the groups of ridges on an apple twig, you can find out how many times the tree has blossomed.

Each apple blossom is held in a small green cup called a *calyx*. When you see the calyx from above, it looks like a star because it has five pale green pointy *lobes*, or *sepals*, that surround the flower. As you will see, five is a very important number for apples.

The sweet-scented apple blossom is a thing of great beauty. But it is much more than that, for it is also an apple factory. Each blossom has five petals that are pink on the outside, white inside, and have a slightly crumpled look. Its bright color and odor attract many bees, and bees help make more apples by spreading pollen.

As bees fly from tree to tree collecting nectar from a blossom here and a blossom there, their hairy bodies become covered with pollen. Each time a bee enters a flower, its hairs pick up a little new pollen, and at the same time, a little of the old pollen falls off. This is important because apples need to be fertilized by pollen of a variety different from their own.

Of course, in order for an apple blossom to become fertilized at all, the pollen has to land in the right place. By examining a blossom carefully, it is easy to see how it all works. If we look closely at the center, we can see many greenish-white threads of different lengths. These are *stamens* and their pale yellow tops are *anthers*. The stamens are attached to the rim of the calyx cup. They are the male organs of the flower and their anthers are covered with the pollen that bees spread.

Also in the center of the blossom we can see the female organs, the *pistils*. There are five

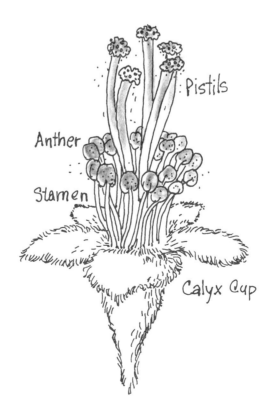

pale-green silky threads called *styles* and each style is topped by a tiny green knob, the *stigma*. It is the stigma that must be fertilized by pollen. Because it is perched right on top of the slender style, a bee can hardly miss brushing against it. The bottom end of the style reaches all the way down into the calyx cup and forms the *ovary*. If all goes well, within a few months the calyx cup will become the juicy white pulp of an apple and the five pistils will become the five cells that snugly hold the apple seeds in place in the core.

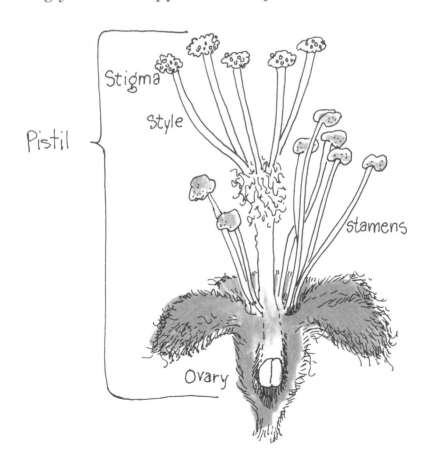

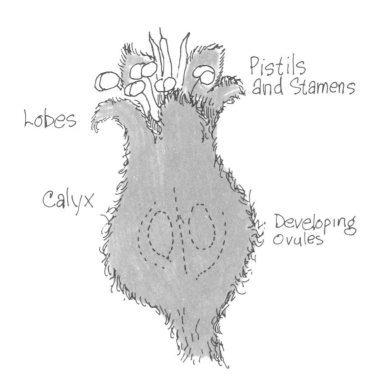

Pistils and Stamens

Lobes

Calyx

Developing Ovules

This is how it happens. As the blossoms open all the way, their undersides no longer show and they appear to be pure white. Then the petals fall to the ground, but the stamens and pistils stay behind. Under them, the lobes of the calyx are still spread out like a five-pointed star but, in a short time, they will draw together and close to form a tube. This happens to only one or two of the blossoms on the end of each twig, but each time it does, an apple is on its way.

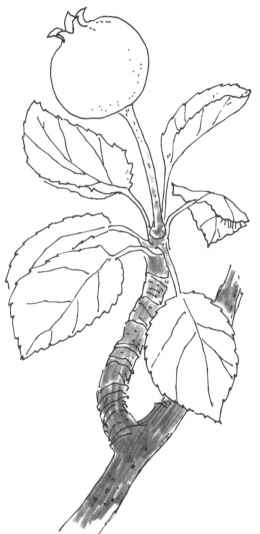

Soon after the calyx
tube is formed, we can
actually see the
beginning tiny green
apple. While just a short
time before, the blossom
was showy and attractive
in order to lure bees,
the small apple is just
as *un*attractive as it can
be. It is the same color
as the leaves and blends
into them so well that it
is almost unnoticeable.
At this stage it is full
of tannic acid which
makes it taste bitter,
and pectin, which makes it
very hard. The starch,
which will later change
to sugar, is indigestible

and is almost certain to give a stomach ache to anyone who eats it. All in all, there is nothing about the young apple that would make anyone want to pick it.

But as soon as the apples are fully ripe, they will once more become attractive with their bright color and inviting perfume.

No living thing has been able to remain on the earth unless it makes more of its own kind, or *reproduces*. An apple tree must be able to make more apples—whether they taste good to humans or not.

When the apples are ripe, so are the seeds. If people or animals eat the fruit then, it is almost certain that some of the seeds will find their way back to the earth and have a chance to grow. It's true that if the apples weren't eaten they would fall to the ground anyway, but then all of the apple trees would sprout in the same place and there wouldn't be enough room for them to grow.

Different kinds of apples take different lengths

of time to mature, but the average is 130 to 145 days after the blossoms appear. When the ripe apple is picked—or has fallen from the tree—a small bud appears near the place where the apple was attached to the tree. It begins to grow outward and soon becomes a whole new twig end. This is the part that will blossom the following spring.

All Kinds of Apples

Even though you recognize an apple when you see one, not all apples look alike. They come in many shades of red, green, yellow, and in mixtures of those colors. They may be perfectly round, oval, or lopsided. Some apples are freckled or blotchy, some are not. Some are as small as golf balls, others as large as softballs. They may feel rough, smooth, waxy, or bumpy. Some have a cloudy "bloom" that rubs off. But there are some things that all apples have in common.

Every apple is covered with skin. The skin may be tough, or so thin and fragile that it is easily bruised. The skin is an important part of the apple because it acts like a coat of armor. The air always carries the bacteria and fungi that cause decay. They cannot reach the apple pulp if the skin is in perfect condition, but if it has even the tiniest break, the apple begins to spoil.

That is why windfall apples—the ones that have fallen from the tree—are rarely good to eat. The fall bruises them and they soon turn brown and mushy.

When you have apples at home, they last longer if you keep them in the refrigerator. Bacteria and fungi do not grow fast at low temperatures.

Another thing that all apples have in common is a dimple at each end. And the ends have names: the top of an apple—the end that was attached to the tree—is called the *stem* end.

Stem end.

Often, the apples you buy still have the stems in place.

The bottom of the apple is the *blossom* end. It is called that because, as the apple grew, the blossom calyx stayed in place and grew right along with the apple. Look at the blossom end of an apple and you will find that the calyx remains are still there. You can easily see the five dried-up lobes. The stamens and styles are still there, too, but they are so withered and shrunken it is hard to find them without a magnifying glass.

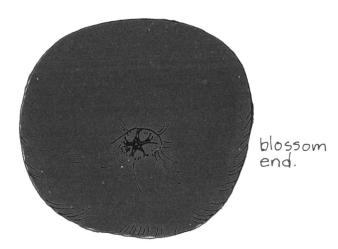

blossom end.

Cut the apple across its middle, between the stem and blossom ends. In the center of each half, there is a beautiful five-pointed star. Each of the five points is a *carpel*—a seed cell—and inside each one there are one or two seeds. Notice that all of the seeds are lined up the same way, with the narrow end pointing toward the stem. Sometimes a seed cell is empty. That means that one stigma of the ovary wasn't fertilized with pollen. Such an apple is often lopsided.

Take out one of the seeds and examine it. It is flat, oval, and only one end is pointy. If you peel off the brown shell, you will find a thin

Enlarged apple seed.

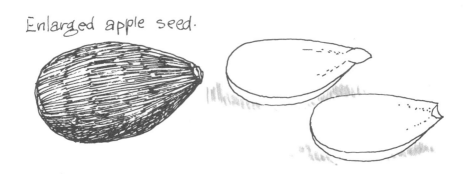

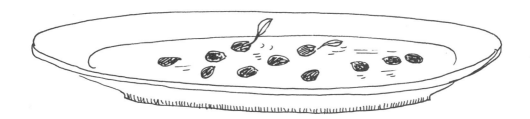

skin underneath. It covers the two white halves
of the seed and protects the *germ*—the part that
will turn into a new plant—which is tucked in
between them.

When the germ begins to grow, it gets its first
food from the white flesh of the seed. After a
while, it puts down roots and gets its
nourishment from the earth.

Keep an apple seed in a little water for a time
and see whether or not the germ grows and sends
out a sprout. If you have no luck, wrap a few
seeds in a damp paper towel and keep them in
a closed plastic bag in the refrigerator for two
weeks. Then take them out and try sprouting
them in water again.

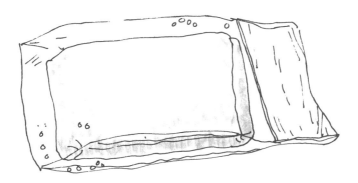

When you looked at the star on an apple half, you probably noticed a circle of ten dots around it. These are the core lines that run lengthwise through the apple. They mark the ten places where bundles of stamens were attached to the rim of the calyx.

Over the centuries, there have been more named varieties of apples than we can count, but today only thirteen varieties make up 90 percent of the commercial apple crop in the United States. Different apples grow better in different parts of the country. And some apples are particularly good for eating while others are better for baking, or for use in pies or applesauce.

Some of our apples got their names from the places they grow, or from the way they look, but others are named for people. One of these is the *Baldwin*, although Mr. Baldwin actually came into the story rather late.

The variety was originally grown by a Massachusetts farmer, John Ball, who had very good luck with a seedling tree around 1740. The red fruit didn't ripen until late in the fall, but then it turned out to be tasty. When Mr. Ball sold his farm to a man

named Butters, he told him about the fine apples. Mr. Butters called the apples *Woodpeckers,* after a family of birds that lived in the tree.

Farmer Butters was generous with scion woods and buds from his splendid tree. Soon all of his friends and neighbors were raising *Woodpeckers.* But about 1784, Colonel Baldwin finally entered the scene. He tasted the apples and decided that they would make a good business. He began to raise the trees and sell them and they soon became known as *Baldwins.* They were especially popular in New York State and for many years, beginning in about 1850, the *Baldwin* was New York's leading commercial apple. Many millions of them were grown, but every single one was a direct descendant of John Ball's lucky seedling.

Baldwin

McIntosh

Another apple named for a person is the *McIntosh*. John McIntosh lived in Ontario, Canada. One day, when he was clearing some land, he found a small clump of apple trees growing from a dropped apple or core. He transplanted the trees so that they would have room to grow, but all of them died except one. That one tree bore remarkable apples.

When Allan, one of the McIntosh sons, grew up, he used that tree to start an apple nursery. Today, McIntosh apples are one of the leading varieties in the United States and in eastern Canada.

Some other very popular varieties are *Delicious, Golden Delicious, Winesap, Jonathan, Rome, York, Imperial, Stayman, Northern Spy,* and *Rhode Island Greening.*

Apples have become big business in the United States. We produce about 150 million bushels a year—85 or 90 apples for every single person in the country!

In addition to being sold fresh, many apples are used in the manufacture of canned applesauce, apple juice, apple pies, and other baked goods. There is also a big market for dried apples, apple cider, and cider vinegar.

It is not surprising that apples are popular, because they taste so good and are nutritious besides. They contain pectin, Vitamins A and C, and some Vitamin B-complex. Their fruit sugar is a source of quick energy and, because apples are about 84 percent water, they are refreshing when you are thirsty. They are easy to store and can be prepared in many delicious ways.

Red Delicious

Golden Delicious

Winesap

Jonathan

Rome Beauty

York Imperial

Stayman

Rhode Island Greening

Apple Myths & Legends

Since apples have been grown by man for thousands of years, it is not surprising that they turn up often in some of the oldest legends handed down to us. Perhaps the most familiar story of all is the one about Eve tempting Adam with an apple in the Garden of Eden. Almost everyone knows about that, but the Bible doesn't *say* it was an apple.

The King James Bible says that when Eve saw "that the tree was good for food, and that it was pleasant to the eyes, and a tree to be desired to make one wise, she took of the fruit thereof, and did eat." Most people have just taken it for granted that the fruit was an apple, but some experts think it was more likely an apricot.

Greek and Roman mythology are rich in apple stories, and in these they really *are* apples, but apples made of gold. One story has to do with the start of the Trojan War, an event that took place a thousand years before the birth of Christ.

It began when the gods of Olympus gave a banquet and didn't invite Eris, the Goddess of Discord. She was angry and decided to make trouble, which happened to be her specialty. During the banquet, she tossed a golden apple

into the hall. It was marked: "For the fairest."
Naturally, all of the goddesses thought it was
meant for them, but finally, the choice was
narrowed down to three—Aphrodite, Hera, and
Pallas Athena. It became clear that they would
never settle the matter among themselves, so
they asked Zeus, the supreme ruler of the gods,
to choose the fairest. But Zeus was far too wise
to get into their argument. Instead, he told them
to ask the young prince Paris, who was supposed
to be a great judge of beauty.

Since each of the goddesses was determined to win the golden apple, they didn't ask Paris to judge fairly, but secretly offered him bribes. Hera offered to make him ruler of all Europe and Asia. Athena promised that he would be able to lead the Trojans in victorious battle against the Greeks. And Aphrodite offered him Helen of Troy, the fairest woman in the world, as his bride. Paris gave Aphrodite the golden apple.

But there was a problem. Helen of Troy was already married to Menelaus, King of Sparta, in Greece. Paris went off to visit the royal couple, who received him cordially. Then Menelaus had to go away, and the ungrateful Paris simply carried Helen off to his home in Troy. When Menelaus came home and found his wife gone, the result was a long and bloody war between the Trojans and the Greeks. By the time it ended, Troy was destroyed, all of the Trojans were dead, and Helen and her husband, Menelaus, were at last reunited.

The greatest of the Greek heroes was Hercules, the strongest man in the world. In one of his many adventures, he was supposed to get, for King Eurystheus of Mycenae, the Golden Apples of the Hesperides, named for the sisters who guarded them.

Atlas, who carried the entire world on his shoulders, was the father of the Hesperides, so Hercules went to ask him if he would fetch the apples. Atlas was tired of holding up the world and quickly said he would be happy to get the apples if Hercules would just hold his burden while he was gone. Hercules agreed, and slipped the world onto his own shoulders.

In time, Atlas returned with the apples, but he
didn't feel like taking the world on his back
again. He told Hercules to keep it and he would
deliver the apples to Eurystheus himself.
Hercules saw that he had been tricked, but
immediately thought of a trick of his own. He
asked Atlas if he would hold the world for just
a moment while he put a pad across his aching
shoulders. Atlas agreed, and as soon as he took
the world, Hercules picked up the apples and
walked off. Both men had strong muscles, but
Hercules clearly had more wit.

Still one more golden apple story concerns
Atalanta, the first great woman athlete, who was
famed in mythology for her skill in hunting,
shooting, and wrestling. Many young men
wanted to marry her, and she finally agreed to
marry anyone who could beat her in a foot race.
Atalanta didn't want to get married at all and
she felt certain that she wouldn't have to,
because no one could run as fast as she could.

But once again brains won out over brawn, for

Atalanta was not outrun, but she *was* outwitted. Hippomenes (also known as Melanion) got hold of three exquisite golden apples. He carried them as he began to race Atalanta. She pulled far ahead of him in the first seconds of the race. Then Hippomenes rolled one of the golden apples in front of her. She took a moment to pick up the beautiful apple and, in that time, Hippomenes reached her side. When she pulled ahead again, he rolled another apple. By his careful timing, and because of Atalanta's greed, she lost the race. Perhaps she was very silly—or who knows?—perhaps she really wanted to get married after all.

Apples in the Kitchen

It's fun to cook with apples, and even more fun to eat what you make. Here are a few apple recipes for you to try, *but if you don't have an electric stove, ask a grownup to light the top of the stove or the oven for you.*

Caramel Apples

You will need for four people:

4 medium-sized, tart, hard, eating apples
½ pound vanilla caramels
4 saved-up lollypop or ice-pop sticks (or ask a
    butcher to sell you 4 wooden skewers)
1 double boiler
1 spoon
wax paper or a dinner plate

1. Put some water in the bottom of the double boiler and put it on the stove to boil. There should be enough water so that the top pan will touch it when you are ready to set it inside, but not so much that it leaks over the sides.

2. While you are waiting for the water to boil, unwrap the caramels and put them into the smaller pan.

3. Wash and dry the apples, remove any stems, and push the sticks into the stem ends.

4. Set the pan of caramels over the boiling water. When they begin to melt, stir them every few minutes. The mixture is not completely melted until it is shiny and very easy to stir. When it reaches that stage, turn off the heat, but leave the caramel pan in the hot water.

5. Hold each apple by its stick over the pan and spoon the hot caramel over the apple, spreading it with the spoon to cover all the bare spots. *Be very careful not to touch the hot caramel. It can cause a bad burn.* If the caramel begins to

thicken, turn the heat on again and stir until it's easy.

6. When each apple is coated, set it, stick up, on a piece of wax paper, or on a plate, to harden.

Apple Crisp

You will need for 8 people:

7 or 8 good cooking apples
½ lemon
1 cup flour
1 cup brown sugar
½ cup (1 stick) margarine or butter, at room
  temperature, so that it is soft
a few grains of salt
1 teaspoon cinnamon
1 medium-sized bowl
1 square baking pan, 7 x 7 or 8 x 8 inches

1. Turn on the oven, set to 375°F.

2. Wash, peel, and slice the apples.

3. Spread the slices evenly in the pan and sprinkle them with the juice of half a lemon.

4. Put all the other ingredients into the bowl and mix them with your fingertips until they are thoroughly blended and crumbly.

5. Sprinkle the mixture evenly over the apple slices.

6. Put the pan into the oven and bake for 30 minutes, or until the apples feel tender when you stick them with a fork.

Serve hot or cold.

Apple Pancakes

You will need for 4 people:

1 cup pancake mix

1 egg
milk { Most pancake mixes call for egg and milk. Read the label to find out how much you need for 1 cup of mix.

butter or margarine
1 or 2 apples
1 skillet
1 pancake turner
powdered sugar

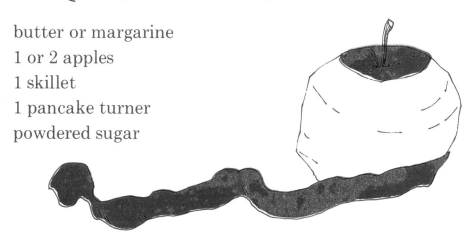

1. Wash, peel, and thinly slice the apple or apples.

2. Mix the pancake mix according to the package directions.

3. Heat the skillet and melt about 1 teaspoon butter or margarine in it.

4. Pour in pancake batter to make pancakes the size you want.

5. Sprinkle a layer of apples on top of each pancake and pour a little more pancake batter over the apples.

6. Use the pancake turner to lift an edge of a pancake so that you can see underneath. When the bottom is brown, flip it over. Add more butter or margarine to the pan if the cakes begin to stick.

7. When the second side is brown, slide the pancakes onto a plate and sprinkle them with powdered sugar.

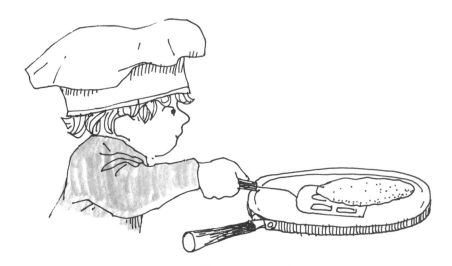

Oven Applesauce

You will need for 6 people:

6 apples
½ cup sugar
½ cup water
1 baking dish with cover
lemon juice, cinnamon, or nutmeg, if you like

1. Turn on the oven, set to 325°F.

2. Peel the apples and cut them in quarters. Cut out the cores and put the apples into the baking dish.

3. Sprinkle the sugar and water over them.

4. Cover the dish and bake until the apples are so soft you can easily mash them with a fork. As you mash, you may add a dash of lemon juice, cinnamon, or nutmeg—or all three.

Serve cold.

Apple Cake

You will need for 6 people:

package of coffee-cake mix—the kind that comes
    with its own foil baking pan and a plastic
    mixing bag
1 egg
¾ cup of applesauce
½ apple

1. Set the oven and follow the mixing directions
according to the recipe on the package, but do
not use any milk; use the applesauce instead.

2. When you have sprinkled the crumb mixture
over the cake batter, slice the apple and arrange
the slices in a pretty design on top of the cake.

3. Bake for 30 minutes—5 minutes longer than
the package recipe calls for.

Index

Adam, 44
America, apples in, 5, 6, 8, 16
animals, and wild apples, 15-16
anthers, 27
Aphrodite, 47-48
apple cake, 62
apple crisp, 58-59
apple pancakes, 59-60
apples, where grown, 5, 40, 41;
   origins of, 5-6;
   uses of, 5, 10, 38, 42, 56-62;
   spread of, 8-9;
   growth of, 24-32;
   young, 30-31;
   maturing of, 32;
   differences among, 33;
   decay of, 34;
   varieties of, 38-42;
   number produced, 42;
   value of, 42;
   golden, 44-45;
   caramel, 56-58;
   see also, tree, apple
applesauce, 61
Appleseed, Johnny, 10, 23
Asia, Southwest, apples from, 5
Atalanta, 53-55
Athena, *see* Pallas Athena
Atlas, 51-53

Babylon, apples and, 5
bacteria, 34
Baldwin, Colonel, 39-40
Baldwins, 39-40
Ball, John, 39-40
bark, of apple tree, 13
beans, planting of, 16
bees, and apple trees, 25-26, 28
Bible, 44
blossom end, 35, 36
blossoms, 14-15, 24-30
branches, of apple tree, 14
budding, 21-22
buds, 24, 32
Butters, Mr., 40

cake, apple, 62
Caesar, Julius, and apples, 6
California, orchards in, 9
calyx, 25, 27-30, 35, 38
cambium, 19
caramel apples, 56-58
carpel, 36
Chapman, John, *see* Appleseed,
   Johnny
China, apples and, 5
cleft-graft, 18-20
colonists, and apples, 6, 8, 10, 18
core, 28, 38
crabapple tree, 13
crisp, apple, 58-59

dimples, 34
dwarf apple tree, 13

England, apples in, 6
Eris, 46-47
Europe, apples and, 5
Eurystheus, King, 50, 53
Eve, 44

family, of apple tree, 14-15
fertilization, 26, 28, 36
fungi, 34

Garden of Eden, 44
germ, 37
grafting, 18-23

Hallowe'en, and apples, 5
head, of apple tree, 13, 20, 22
Helen of Troy, 48-49
Hera, 47-48
Hercules, 50-53
Hesperides, 50-51
Hippomenes, 55
hybrids, 17-18

Indians, and apples, 9, 10

Jefferson, Thomas, and apples, 8

leaves, apple, 13-14
legends, 44-55
life, of apple tree, 23
lobes, *see* sepals

Massachusetts Bay Colony, apples
    in, 6
McIntosh apples, 41
McIntosh, John and Allan, 41
Melanion, 55
Menelaus, 49
myths, 44-55

New Amsterdam, *see* New York City
New World, *see* America
New York City, apple tree in, 7, 16
New York State, Baldwins in, 40
nursery, apple, 23

Olympus, gods of, 46
ovary, 28, 36
oven applesauce, 61

Pallas Athena, 47-48
pancakes, apple, 59-60
Paris, 47-49
pioneers, and apples, 8, 18, 23
pistils, 27-29
pollen, 25-26, 28, 36

recipes, apples, 56-62

sayings, about apples, 5
scion, 18-21
seeds, 36-37;
    planting of, 6, 10, 16-18;
    ripening of, 31
sepals, 25, 29, 35
settlers, *see* colonists
size, of apple tree, 13
skin, of apples, 34
stamens, 27, 29, 35, 38
stem, 34-36
stigma, 28, 36
Stone Age, apples and, 5

strength, of apple tree, 14
Stuyvesant, Peter, and apple
    tree, 7, 16

tree, apple, 10, 13-23;
    wild, 15-16;
    uses of, 23;
    blossoming of, 24
Trojan War, 46-49
trunk, of apple tree, 13
twigs, 24, 32

Virginia, apples in, 8

Washington, George, and apples, 8
West, seeds and trees to, 8, 23
windfalls, 34
wood, apple, uses of, 23
Woodpeckers, 40

Zeus, 47

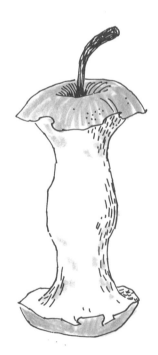